Garfield loses his feet

BY: JIM DAVIS

BALLANTINE BOOKS · NEW YORK

Library of Congress Catalog Card Number: 84-90814
ISBN 0-345-31805-6

Manufactured in the United States of America

First Edition: October 1984

20   19   18   17   16   15   14   13   12

GARFIELD: ©1978 United Feature Syndicate, Inc.

COME ON, MONDAY! DO IT TO ME NOW! THE SUSPENSE IS KILLING ME!

JIM DAVIS   3-21

TH'OCK

© 1983 United Feature Syndicate, Inc.

THANK YOU FOR YOUR PROMPT CONSIDERATION

DID I EVER TELL YOU ABOUT MY UNCLE NICK? HE LOVES TO DESTROY THINGS. HE CAN SHRED A RECLINER IN 12 SECONDS...

3-22   JIM DAVIS

MANGLE FERNS BY THE CARLOAD AND TURN A SET OF CHINA INTO POWDER IN THE BLINK OF AN EYE

HE IS PRESENTLY A POSTAL EMPLOYEE IN CHICAGO

© 1983 United Feature Syndicate, Inc.

PUNT

3-28

THIS IS TURNING OUT TO BE A DECENT MONDAY FOR A CHANGE

© 1983 United Feature Syndicate, Inc. JIM DAVIS

POOMP!

GOBBLE GOBBLE GOBBLE

GARFIELD

JIM DAVIS

3-29

GARFIELD, YOU EAT TOO FAST

NO, I DON'T

GARFIELD

© 1983 United Feature Syndicate, Inc.

I'M JUST OVERQUALIFIED FOR THE JOB

GARFIELD

JRM DAVIS

4·3

© 1983 United Feature Syndicate, Inc.

WE MUST HAVE LUNCH SOMETIME

THINGS AREN'T ALWAYS AS THEY SEEM

HEY, GARFIELD, LET'S TAKE A VACATION

JIM DAVIS

WE'LL GO SOMEPLACE TROPICAL

4-4

SAVE YOUR MONEY. GO SIT IN YOUR AQUARIUM

© 1983 United Feature Syndicate, Inc.

VACATION IS GOING TO BE SO GREAT, GARFIELD

JIM DAVIS

4-5

WE'LL GET AWAY FROM THIS RAT RACE. THERE'LL BE NO HASSLES

A CHANGE OF PACE WOULD BE NICE

© 1983 United Feature Syndicate, Inc.

THE CAPTAIN HAS ADVISED THAT THE "FASTEN SEAT BELT" SIGN BE OBSERVED IN CASE SOME SLIGHT AIR TURBULENCE IS ENCOUNTERED

WELL, GARFIELD, HOW DID YOU LIKE YOUR FIRST AIRPLANE RIDE?

ASIDE FROM THE NAUSEA, CRAMPS AND INDIGESTION, I'M FINE

HAVE A NICE DAY

HAVE A NICE DAY?!

LET HER LIVE, GARFIELD! LET HER LIVE!

Dear Garfield,
What is your favorite
all-time film?

4-25   JIM DAVIS

IT'S "OLD YELLER"

© 1983 United Feature Syndicate, Inc.

I LOVE MOVIES
WITH HAPPY
ENDINGS

JIM DAVIS   4-26

© 1983 United Feature Syndicate, Inc.

AND JUST WHAT DO YOU
THINK YOU'RE DOING?

ASSERTING MY
CATHOOD?

WHY DO YOU HAVE SUCH LARGE TEETH, GARFIELD?

JIM DAVIS 4-29

ALL THE BETTER TO EAT YOU WITH, MY DEAR

STOP THAT!

OBVIOUSLY, SIR, YOU ARE NOT A PATRON OF THE CLASSICS

© 1983 United Feature Syndicate, Inc.

I SAW AN AWFUL MOVIE LAST NIGHT CALLED "ALIEN DOG." IT WAS ABOUT THIS GIGANTIC MUTT THAT TERRORIZED THE WORLD

JIM DAVIS 4-30

HOWEVER, THEY DID DISPATCH HIM WITH A RATHER CLEVER PLOY

THEY ELECTRIFIED A 12-STORY FIRE HYDRANT

© 1983 United Feature Syndicate, Inc.

LET'S PUT THIS WHOLE THING IN PERSPECTIVE

EATING IS IMPORTANT

JIM DAVIS

5-1

AND SLEEPING IS IMPORTANT

© 1983 United Feature Syndicate, Inc.

BUT NOTHING IS MORE IMPORTANT THAN HOLDING SOMEONE YOU LOVE

CHECK THAT

RECIPROCATION IS NICE, TOO

OH, NO! MY WATCH HAS STOPPED!

I'VE MISSED GARFIELD'S MEALTIME

PETS HAVE A WAY OF LETTING YOU KNOW WHEN YOU'VE MISSED THEIR MEALTIME

YOU'RE LATE

I KNOW. I KNOW

JIM DAVIS

5-8

TELL ME, GARFIELD, WHEN YOU WALK, DO YOUR RIGHT AND LEFT LEGS TRAVEL TOGETHER, OR DO YOU USE YOUR OPPOSING LEGS?

JIM DAVIS

© 1983 United Feature Syndicate, Inc.

I'LL NEVER WALK AGAIN

5-9

I WONDER HOW BIRDS CAN SLEEP IN TREES WITHOUT FALLING OUT

JIM DAVIS   5-10

AHA!... HAMMOCKS

© 1983 United Feature Syndicate, Inc.

THAT'S ODD... TWO LITTLE BUGS IN FULL SHAKESPEAREAN DRESS

ROMEO, ROMEO, WHEREFORE ART THOU, ROMEO?

I'M RIGHT HERE, JULIET

I BRING BAD NEWS, JULIE BABY. OUR FAMILIES ARE FEUDING AND DON'T WANT US TO DATE ANYMORE

OH NO!

THAT DOES IT! LET'S DIE IN EACH OTHER'S ARMS AND LIVE TOGETHER IN ETERNITY

HOW DO WE DO THAT?

JIM DAVIS   5-22

HERE'S HOW

SQUASH

I'M NOT ONE TO FOOL WITH GREAT LITERATURE

© 1983 United Feature Syndicate, Inc.

5·29

© 1983 United Feature Syndicate, Inc.

JIM DAVIS

I'M GOING OUT TO A VERY NICE RESTAURANT TONIGHT, GARFIELD. SO YOU BE GOOD WHILE I'M GONE

JIM DAVIS 5-30

AND, NO, YOU CAN'T COME WITH ME

© 1983 United Feature Syndicate, Inc.

WHO SAID I WANTED TO GO TO YOUR CRUMMY RESTAURANT, ANYWAY?

JON IS GOING OUT WITHOUT US TONIGHT, ODIE

JIM DAVIS 5-31

SO YOU KNOW WHAT TO DO...

YOU CHEW HIS SLIPPERS AND I'LL DESTROY HIS CHAIR

© 1983 United Feature Syndicate, Inc.

SQUIRT

OKAY! WHO GREASED MY WIENER?!

© 1983 United Feature Syndicate, Inc.

HEY, GARFIELD, WHAT DO YOU THINK OF THE NEW TURTLENECK SWEATER MOM MADE YOU?

YOU'RE RIGHT

IT ISN'T VERY FLATTERING, IS IT?

© 1983 United Feature Syndicate, Inc.

GARFIELD, MEET MY NEW PET FROG, "HERBIE"

ISN'T HE GREAT?

YEH, GOOD OL' "HERBIE"

GOOD OL' "YOUR DAYS ARE NUMBERED AS SOON AS JON TURNS HIS BACK, HERBIE"

JIM DAVIS · 6-8

JIM DAVIS · 6-9

© 1983 United Feature Syndicate, Inc.

HEY, GARFIELD! LET'S HAVE SOME FUN!

FORGET IT, JON

I WANT TO TAKE YOU TO AN ITALIAN RESTAURANT FOR A LASAGNA DINNER

NO WAY

JIM DAVIS

6-12

THEY HAVE FERNS FOR DESSERT

BIG DEAL

THEN WE CAN COME HOME AND I'LL HOLD ODIE DOWN WHILE YOU BEAT HIM UP

TRY AND MAKE ME

© 1983 United Feature Syndicate, Inc.

HOW DID YOU KNOW WE HAVE AN APPOINTMENT AT THE VET'S?

I DON'T KNOW. I JUST KNOW

IN THIS BOX, I HAVE A SINGING AND DANCING MOUSE. I HAVE SPENT FOUR YEARS TRAINING HIM. HE WILL NOW ENTERTAIN YOU

6-13

I GUESS I SHOULD HAVE CUT AIR HOLES IN THE BOX

IT'S HARD TO BELIEVE I'M GOING TO BE FIVE YEARS OLD THIS SUNDAY

JIM DAVIS   6-14

SHUCKS, GOLLY, GEE-WHIZ, RATSO

I'M GOING TO HAVE TO START WATCHING MY LANGUAGE

GARFIELD, I HOPE THE SUN SHINES ON YOUR BIRTHDAY

WHAT A NICE THING TO SAY

JIM DAVIS
6·15

I'M GOING CAMPING

I DIDN'T NEED THAT

JIM DAVIS   6-16

MOTHER NATURE HAS CERTAINLY BEEN KIND TO YOU, GARFIELD

I WISH I COULD SAY THE SAME FOR FATHER TIME

© 1983 United Feature Syndicate, Inc.

THEY SAY THE FIRST THING TO GO ON A CAT IS ITS HEARING

JIM DAVIS 6-17

OR WAS THAT EYESIGHT?

© 1983 United Feature Syndicate, Inc.

YOUR BIRTHDAY GIFT IS INSIDE THIS CARD, GARFIELD

JIM DAVIS 6-18

SOMEDAY, MY SIGNATURE WILL BE WORTH A LOT OF MONEY!

© 1983 United Feature Syndicate, Inc.

AMOEBA MAN STOPS TO ADMIRE HIMSELF IN THE MIRROR

JIM DAVIS   6-24

FACE IT, FELLA, YOU'RE ONE GOOD-LOOKING HUNK OF PROTOPLASM

© 1983 United Feature Syndicate, Inc.

JIM DAVIS   6-25

AMOEBA MAN FALLS IN LOVE

IF I MAY BE SO BOLD, YOU HAVE A GREAT-LOOKING PSEUDOPOD, MY DEAR

© 1983 United Feature Syndicate, Inc.

© 1983 United Feature Syndicate, Inc.

7-6

7-7

THERE YOU HAVE IT...

ODIE'S SO STUPID, HE DOESN'T EVEN UNDERSTAND THE LAW OF GRAVITY

7-17

JIM DAVIS

I AM ABOUT TO OUTDO MYSELF

WHAP!

© 1983 United Feature Syndicate, Inc.

WHAT ARE YOU DOING UP HERE? DID YOU COME TO SAVE ME?

JIM DAVIS 7-22

NO, I JUST CAME TO VISIT

WELL, TALK FAST. I WAS JUST CONSIDERING LEAPING TO MY DEATH

© 1983 United Feature Syndicate, Inc.

HOW DO WE GET OUT OF THIS TREE?

WE JUMP

JIM DAVIS 7-23

IF THAT LITTLE TWERP CAN JUMP, SO CAN I

© 1983 United Feature Syndicate, Inc.

GARFIELD, I KNOW YOU'RE IN MY FERN. I CAN SEE YOUR TAIL

WHAT DO YOU HAVE TO SAY FOR YOURSELF?

© 1983 United Feature Syndicate, Inc.

IF YOU MUST KNOW, I AM A RARE CARNIVOROUS FERN, AND IF YOU DON'T MIND, I'D LIKE TO FINISH EATING YOUR CAT IN PEACE

JIM DAVIS   8-1

JIM DAVIS   8-2

HA-HA! YOU DIDN'T GET MY FOOD THAT TIME!

SPLAT

© 1983 United Feature Syndicate, Inc.

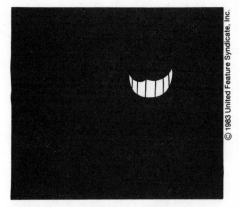

GARFIELD, I WANT YOU TO GET ALL THE MICE OUT OF THIS HOUSE, RIGHT NOW!

OH, VERY WELL

JIM DAVIS   8-5

BE A GOOD BOY AND CALL MY ATTORNEY, WILL YOU?

AND HAVE HIM SERVE THEM WITH AN EVICTION NOTICE

© 1983 United Feature Syndicate, Inc.

JIM DAVIS   8-6

ARRRGH!!!

B-B-B-B!

CATS ARE SO UNPREDICTABLE

PREDICTABLY SO

© 1983 United Feature Syndicate, Inc.

JIM DAVIS 8-8

OH, NO!

© 1983 United Feature Syndicate, Inc.

MY LEGS ARE SHRINKING!

I'VE REALLY DONE IT THIS TIME. MY BELLY HAS OUTGROWN MY LEGS

JIM DAVIS 8-9

I GUESS THERE'S ONLY ONE THING TO DO...

GET FITTED FOR STILTS

© 1983 United Feature Syndicate, Inc.

RIIIP!

CRUELTY IS SECOND NATURE TO THAT CAT

© 1983 United Feature Syndicate, Inc.

DIET TIME

RATS

© 1983 United Feature Syndicate, Inc.

HAPPY DIET, GARFIELD. HERE'S A BANANA FOR BREAKFAST

8-17 JIM DAVIS

BANG!

© 1983 United Feature Syndicate, Inc.

AS LONG AS YOU'RE DIETING, GARFIELD, WHY DON'T YOU EXERCISE, TOO?

JIM DAVIS 8-18

SURE... WHY NOT?

AS LONG AS THE NOOSE IS AROUND MY NECK, I MIGHT AS WELL JUMP OFF THE HORSE

© 1983 United Feature Syndicate, Inc.

JIM DAVIS 8-21

© 1983 United Feature Syndicate, Inc.

THEY SAY WE CAN VISIT HIM 2 TO 4 ON SATURDAYS

FOOD GONE! FOOD ALL GONE!

THAT WASN'T VERY NICE, GARFIELD

IN THIS BUSINESS, "NICE" DOESN'T PUT BREAD ON THE TABLE

WHY IS IT I'M CRAZY ABOUT YOU, GARFIELD?

PROBABLY BECAUSE I'M PERFECT

YOU CLAW THE DRAPES, SHED ON THE FURNITURE, STEAL MY FOOD AND HASSLE THE DOG

NOBODY'S PERFECT

JON MUST BE CLEANING THE HEATING GRATE. I WONDER WHAT GRATES ARE FOR, ANYWAY

JIM DAVIS 9-5

OOPS!

OBVIOUSLY, THEY'RE TO KEEP ONE'S HOUSE FROM EATING ONE'S CAT

SILLY ME HAD TO FALL INTO THE HEATING VENT. NOW HERE I AM, RESIDING DEEP WITHIN THE BOWELS OF MY HOME

JIM DAVIS 9-6

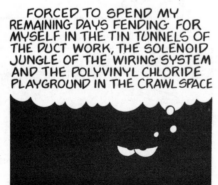

FORCED TO SPEND MY REMAINING DAYS FENDING FOR MYSELF IN THE TIN TUNNELS OF THE DUCT WORK, THE SOLENOID JUNGLE OF THE WIRING SYSTEM AND THE POLYVINYL CHLORIDE PLAYGROUND IN THE CRAWL SPACE

HEY! I THINK THERE'S A BOOK HERE SOMEWHERE

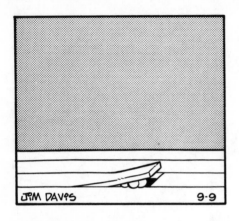

UNNNGH

© 1983 United Feature Syndicate, Inc.

GARFIELD... WHERE ARE YOU?

DOWN HERE IN THE FLOOR JOISTS, PLOTTING YOUR UNTIMELY DEMISE

FREE AT LAST!

THERE IS SOMETHING TO BE SAID FOR BRUTE FORCE

9-10

IT IS USUALLY FOLLOWED BY BRUTE STUPIDITY

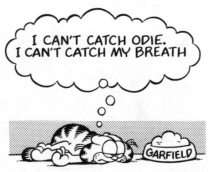

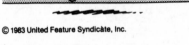

POOKY, I HAVE TO START WEANING MYSELF FROM YOU. I GOTTA MAKE IT OUT THERE ON MY OWN

JIM DAVIS   9-28

THAT'S GOOD ENOUGH FOR THE FIRST WEEK

I HAVE TO BREAK THIS TEDDY BEAR DEPENDENCY

JIM DAVIS   9-29

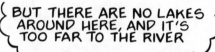

GARFIELD SHOULD BE FINDING THAT RUBBER HOT DOG IN HIS BOWL RIGHT ABOUT NOW

JIM DAVIS   10-7

AND HE SHOULD BE COMING FOR ME RIGHT ABOUT...

© 1983 United Feature Syndicate, Inc.

NOW

I THINK I'LL HAVE PANCAKES FOR BREAKFAST

© 1983 United Feature Syndicate, Inc.

JIM DAVIS   10-8

ONCE AGAIN OUR NATION'S CRIMINAL ELEMENT HAS CALLOUSLY DISREGARDED THE TRUTH IN PACKAGING LAWS

I WISH I COULD KICK THIS INDUSTRIAL-STRENGTH DEPRESSION I HAVE TODAY

JIM DAVIS

10-9

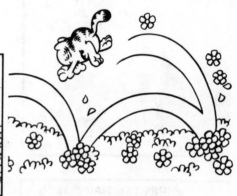

MOTHER NATURE, IF YOU HAD A BODY AND A FACE, I'D GIVE YOU A HUG AND A KISS

© 1983 United Feature Syndicate, Inc.

GARFIELDS YET TO COME!

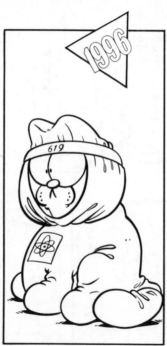